Terra Incognita

Hollis Summers Poetry Prize

GENERAL EDITOR: SARAH GREEN

Named after the distinguished poet who taught for many years at Ohio University and made Athens, Ohio, the subject of many of his poems, this competition invites writers to submit unpublished collections of original poems. The competition is open to poets who have not published a book-length collection as well as to those who have.

Full and updated information is available on the Hollis Summers Poetry Prize web page: ohioswallow.com/poetry_prize.

Meredith Carson, *Infinite Morning*
Memye Curtis Tucker, *The Watchers*
V. Penelope Pelizzon, *Nostos*
Kwame Dawes, *Midland*
Allison Eir Jenks, *The Palace of Bones*
Robert B. Shaw, *Solving for X*
Dan Lechay, *The Quarry*
Joshua Mehigan, *The Optimist*
Jennifer Rose, *Hometown for an Hour*
Ann Hudson, *The Armillary Sphere*
Roger Sedarat, *Dear Regime: Letters to the Islamic Republic*
Jason Gray, *Photographing Eden*
Will Wells, *Unsettled Accounts*
Stephen Kampa, *Cracks in the Invisible*
Nick Norwood, *Gravel and Hawk*
Charles Hood, *South x South: Poems from Antarctica*
Alison Powell, *On the Desire to Levitate*
Shane Seely, *The Surface of the Lit World*
Michelle Y. Burke, *Animal Purpose*
Michael Shewmaker, *Penumbra*
Idris Anderson, *Doubtful Harbor*
Joseph J. Capista, *Intrusive Beauty*
Julie Hanson, *The Audible and the Evident*
Fleda Brown, *Flying through a Hole in the Storm*
Sara Henning, *Terra Incognita*

Terra Incognita

Poems

Sara Henning

OHIO UNIVERSITY PRESS

ATHENS

Ohio University Press, Athens, Ohio 45701
ohioswallow.com
© 2022 by Ohio University Press

To obtain permission to quote, reprint, or otherwise reproduce or distribute
material from Ohio University Press publications, please contact our
rights and permissions department at (740) 593-1154 or (740) 593-4536
(fax).

Printed in the United States of America
Ohio University Press books are printed on acid-free paper ∞ ™

31 30 29 28 27 26 25 24 23 22 21   5 4 3 2 1

Library of Congress Cataloging-in-Publication Data
Names: Henning, Sara, author.
Title: Terra incognita : poems / Sara Henning.
Description: Athens : Ohio University Press, [2022] | Series: Hollis Sum-
mers poetry prize
Identifiers: LCCN 2021032499 (print) | LCCN 2021032500 (ebook) | ISBN
9780821424759 (paperback) | ISBN 9780821447734 (pdf)
Subjects: LCGFT: Poetry.
Classification: LCC PS3608.E564536 T47 2022 (print) | LCC PS3608.
E564536 (ebook) | DDC 811/.6—dc23
LC record available at https://lccn.loc.gov/2021032499
LC ebook record available at https://lccn.loc.gov/2021032500

In memory of my mother,
Debra Louise Henning
(1954–2016)

Contents

IV. Terra Firma

I

Terra Inferna

Before you know what kindness really is
you must lose things,
feel the future dissolve in a moment.

—Naomi Shihab Nye

Terra Inferna

When my mother died, I dreamed of a man
rough-sketching on gesso, palette knife scraping
the angles of a woman's face. He knuckles
thin washes of color, the way a man might thumb
through a woman, exulting her, erasing her.
He's famous for his horses, hunger-hardened
and sensual, pupils blown open by violence
or love. Others thrash with their hooves,
escapists hurling forward. I dreamed
of the teenage girl always ghosting the interior,
cut-off blue jeans, black camisole, smoke
clenching her body in its silt halo. There's a Zippo
next to her, a crushed pack of Lucky Strikes.
Her off-frame stare says, *Listen.* It says, *I want
to tell you everything.* Once, a mare thrust
her muzzle into the shotgun window of his 1967
Chevy Nova — this was years ago — Tulsa,
a whole afternoon of hooky in the field off
Route 66 by the high school. Rabbits, tonguing
the husks off of sweet corn. His back,
sunburned as raw prayer, as the radio pulses
Van Morrison. The girl in the back seat,
offering him her body. The mare's face
in the window is a flash, a sudden weapon.
She could break the young man reaching for her,
crush his hands with her jaw. She could bite
the girl until her skin gapes and slips,
flesh pooling in plush knots. I think of this image
when I close my eyes — a girl so lovely
it hurts to look at her, a mare wild enough

to end everything, a mane that smells
like sex, prairie fire, rabbits seething
their death song into the glare. The man
will call it some heart's undoing, as if
to repeat the thing you most want will keep it
holy. Like the night his girl falls asleep,
her cigarette glimmering. He won't be able
to unsee it—her soul lunging its muscled heat
into air, screams chased down by darkness.
Or the mare, always the mare—feral elegy
he'll snare into oil, her mane so light-tangled
it could be burning.

Elegy with Saltwater Taffy

River Street Sweets, Savannah, Georgia, 1984

You could say we came, my mother and I,
to watch the aproned man pour his tincture
of cornstarch and sugar onto the metal table,
wait until it hardened enough to be touched.
You could say we waited for him to move
it to the stretching machine, to wrestle
and press the melon spice candy against
the iron arms. You could say it amazed us,
the physics of it, how something so simple
could soften and harden like the whims
of the body. We watched him conjure
taffy into snakelike ropes, feed it
into a hundred-year-old machine which cut,
then folded each piece into wax paper.
But really, we came for the pieces
he flung at us, how they arched in parabolas
or shot like fastballs over our heads.
I loved it when I could catch one —
warmth still radiating, paper skin,
the shape my mouth made around it.
And after, I'd beg my mother to walk
by the river until my flip-flops burned
the ridge between my toes, seagulls scattering
when we came too close. Even now,
I relish the salt and sugar still kindling
together, sweat-luscious body and taffy.
I can still taste the sea.

Queening

When our calico Manx
    seizes up like the women at Auntie's church
        who writhe at the pulpit,

      moan the name of Jesus,
    my mother says she's *queening*.
Exhausted on her floral towel,

she licks herself in the laundry room
    near the water heater, amniotic sac
        enclosing a kitten like iridescent burlap.

      My mother grasps each tiny, wet
    body that comes, cuts the umbilical cord
with scissors, ties off the placental

scrim with dental floss. When she ceases
    to pant and squat, we believe they've all
      come, two toms squalling

      from a heating pad. Hours later,
    one more will crest from her pelvic canal
into the litter box. We won't find her

until her mother's yowling draws us
    out of bed. When we cut
      the runt Manx free, she struggles

      to breathe. All day, I watch her
    throng her mother for milk,
eyes still sealed. Outside our house,

children haunt the streets
    in Tang-stained T-shirts.
        A splintering telephone pole leans

        into the crush. Birds gliding
    on electrical wire Houdini into air.
I envy their brief mirage,

their reckless miracle, the cat
    nimble around my mother's
        ankles as she turned the deadbolt

        last April, estrus cycle driving the cat
    to the heated canopy of azalea
bushes. Her scruff bitten by feral tom

after feral tom, the spines
    on each penis triggering her ovulation.
        When she called to be let in,

        the morula was already forming.
    What intrigues me are the cells migrating
in the body long after birth, fetal cells

joining the mother's aortic surges,
    her brain's neurotransmitters,
        the individual platelets in her blood.

        Microchimerism, scientists call it,
    when really mother and child
have bonded beyond their bones.

Cells, instinctual and rootless,
    tessellating the body like the smooth,
        beige throats of beer bottles

smashed in the street,
the way my mother stepped through
them to reach our front door,

my head pressed to her hip,
our shadows fused to the glass flash.
Years later, after tumors shudder

inside her like a field of blown
honeydew melons, I wonder if her
love still lurks inside me, dark

as placenta or the cats of my childhood,
lusty boys delivered between
tongued interludes, the lone

female who slipped free
from her mother. As with my grief,
we found homes for the healthy,

kept the bird-boned queen
who learned to sleep on my chest
at night. Like the cells that bind us,

we welcomed her as our own.

Mom's Eggs

It's the glistening I can't unsee now — her eggs
slipped fast into margarine. Naked, something
indecent miring the interior of Teflon.
My mother, thirty, palms a plastic spatula

as albumen clouds the hot skillet. My first
memory — two martyrs cracked open, their future
braised slow. Years later, I'm still fork-deep
in awakening. She's dead, and no one can teach me

to pierce the grief, to catch its trigger of salt.
It's a feat I can't master — that sweet spot pulsing hard,
then raw. Supple under a trick of silk,

her effigy bristles, burns. How she loved me.
I fry my eggs as if I can taste her, savor what I
can scrape: I eat my failing. I kill the heat.

Elegy Beginning with the Birth of a Mountain

White County, Georgia

You believe that a mountain comes gaunt and shivering, some
sleek brute borne from the void of Chaos. When you close your
eyes, you can almost see it—each salt-glossed body rapturing
itself up from the earth. Giant cow elks birthed in the middle of a
gorge. You beg your mother to drive the hour to White County so
you can linger at the Chevron station, staring at mountains and
drinking Cokes. Around you, farmhouses lean into the September
heat. They haunt the landscape, derelict, all plank and radiant
tin. Cemeteries go rogue on the side of the road. You didn't know
that to love a mountain is to hold a language of violence in your
mouth—tectonic plates gashing each other, hot magma, erosion.
You aren't that kind of child. *The animal-sky,* you once said, *is love
turned inside out.* You are ready to coil your fingers around your
binoculars, to believe in a field of view inversely proportional to
their magnifying power. Ready to believe in their angular value,
how many degrees will hold you and for how long. What you see—
ridges erased by haze. Oaks, heat-threatened, radiating isoprene.
Gas smattering the sky. Like the trees, you're seized between beauty
and blue's hazard, the ridge's tawny girth and the surge of the soul,
so nakedly rising it could be joy or sadness. Remember, you once
called the sky *dusk-raw.* Later, you'll want a world where tumors in
your mother's body mean proud mountains move within her.

God of the Kitchen Window

It hovered all June next to my mother's
Our Lady of Guadalupe candles—

the toothpick-pierced avocado seed,
half-hung in a Ziggy coffee cup. I felt

like Longinus, watching the little god
burst through its seed coat, cotyledon

flaring like a calf's skull, roots unfurled
from all ends. I imagined our Maytag dryer

lulling it to sleep as it churned through
its rebirth, so princely above the sink

of cereal bowls and egg-scorched pans.
At night, lights from Cedar Shoals

High School's stadium lit up our yard,
staining it the color of skim milk.

From earth that gave her azaleas
like starved, plucked chickens, their roots

lashing through clay, did she expect
the pit, like magic beans, to angle

through air, cling to the cirrus clouds,
their wet, stretched calico? Would she

have climbed the stalk to find a heaven
full of ripe avocados, their flesh

glinting shyly in the air? So many times,
I watched her lean against our kitchen

counter, slice the skin of an avocado,
spoon the flesh right into her mouth.

When mold, like drupes of olives,
pearled through the water, I knew

it was over. My mother longed
for an avocado tree to spread its leaves

in her backyard, because in some
small way, she still loved the world.

I watched her bury it, that misfit pit,
the way she buried my father.

French Fries

When I say lesions in my mother's lungs / knot the CT scan
　　like a field / of thistle

I mean she's haunting the drive-through / at the nearest
　　Krystal / a grease-slick bag

of french fries enchanting the air / I mean a nurse / stitched up
　　the port in her chest

where chemo once flooded / dressed the site with surgical
　　glue / her throat closing over

the word *terminal* / when I was young, hard days meant / cruising
　　after school

with a fast-food sack between us / my mother tearing
　　the paper / to cool the shards

of fever-slick spud / we'd crush with our molars / exhaust
　　from the muffler thrumming

through the windows / magnolia murmuring its sweet, ripe
　　song / through us

I want to remember her like this / radio blaring / mother
　　grasping fries like slivers

of pleasure / miles soaked in the heat bleach of bird
　　bones / that illicit salt

Smoking in the Car

In the belly of every summer day is a god
taking its first breath, so I learn to call it praying,
my mother forsaking the AC for a grace called *smoking
in the car*. I watch her pry the window's handle

as it jams midcrank, clench the sultry juts
of plastic scorching her palms. I watch her jimmy it,
the glass that will blast only hot air at us,
then pull on a spit-glazed filter, her dusky exhale

ribboning through the car. Each hit a blitz
of nicotine. A prophesy of what's to come.
I watch her brake, then brandish her arm,

her body a human seatbelt touching my skin.
I close my eyes. I steady myself in my seat.
From another car over, I look like I'm on my knees.

Cancer

Emory Saint Joseph's Hospital, Atlanta, Georgia

Still flushed on dreams and the stark scrim of sleep, her call
    tears me awake—1 a.m. *Honey, we*
are in trouble, she says. *Someone took me.* My mother's slurs
    are the siren call of real

stolen women: first a strange man ties her with rope, then drugs
    her. He eases his cool
weapon too close to her throat. She says, *Oh God, he's coming.*
    She says, *If we*

hurry, he might not kill me. Her voice retethers her grip, as if I
    never left
the country of her body. Our relationship—twenty years too
    late. My only school

of thought now is guilt, that animal trigger. Fear, my translu-
    cent temple. *Honey, we*
need you to drive. He slashed her favorite purse, she says—
    I can't mistake the lurk

of exposure in her tone. *He's got my keys. I'm too scared*
    to move. The sheriff is late
picking up our three-way call. To track her GPS, he says,
    my mother must dial 911. We

have no choice but to cut her line. Dread shushes its hot lien
    against me. He says, *Strike*
first, then move. But what if her abductor jumps her mid-dial,
    coldcocks her straight

before she reaches the cops? What if he's already on his way
    to rape her? *We*
will do what we can, he says. Hangs up. I sit on the floor, my pulse
    in my throat. I'm sing-

led out. I'd joined the sisterhood of bad daughters years ago,
    traitor women. My sin
my inability to save my mother or my soul. A half hour later,
    the sheriff calls—*We*

found her. No rapist in sight, no man shifting everything
    to bruise: instead, Dilaudid thin-
ning her post-op pain. Half of her liver knifed out by surgeons.
    Cancer, like gin

in her blood, turning everything smooth. Stage four. Meta-
    static. Who can we
turn to in moments like this? Gary, the night oncology nurse,
    his voice like deep jazz?

My mother, midhallucination, speed-dialing me from ICU?
    Last June,
a tumor ate through her colon, ovaries, the slick gloss of her
    uterine walls. *We*

are this alibi of blood muscled down, Mother. A legacy plying
    the deep. To die,
to sleep—what's thicker than devotion? Love flown too soon.

Here Be Dragons

Turtle Island Preserve Educational Camp, Boone,
North Carolina, 1989

Imagine our cells are pilgrims, envoys to our darkest longitudes.
Imagine I'm swimming in a lake of DNA, destiny blazed up all around me:
wraiths of future selves stalking the sandy beach of the soul.

My father, dead at thirty-six. My aunt's knees slit into crosses,
titanium fusing each interior joint. Imagine I'm nine again, summer camp,

gazing as turtles sun their bodies in the brush, the Iroquois myth
turning to flesh in front of me. A turtle, a great flood looming.
With her body, she started a world. But there, tangled in the soak,

I see her, the wounded one, her shell another earth jagged open.
Like her, my cells could unfurl their shadows into the cool. Like her,

I could learn to wade toward the shore of my ending, all angle
and seizing heat, rocks so slick I would catch at anything not to fall.
I could be a tempest in space, my heels undulating as I skin my palms.

I watch the sun hush the stars invisible, their moving braille
hazed until another night takes us. I watch my future open, then close.

I read somewhere that dark matter binds our galaxies to one another,
but as a child I slept through each planet muscled into anonymous
circuits, their glide like starlight in my blood. Later, I'd think of sphinx

moths clung to a silhouette of water when tumors spread through
my mother's body. When she died in her sleep, her breath flickered

into cadence, that constant hum—wings twisting into silence.
But I long to believe she's that turtle, cracked like cathedral glass,
her dying body helixing down. I'm so sick of it, projecting.

Sometimes a turtle is just a turtle. A mother just a mother.
Sometimes blood, like love, is how we survive each other.

II

Terra Incognita

Why does that strange sea make no sound?
Is it because we're far away?

—Elizabeth Bishop

Terra Incognita

Grief doesn't have a face like
the living do. But that doesn't keep

me from wanting the ocean,
like a god, to take me in its mouth —

my skin salt-thrashed, the whole
of me eaten through by riptide.

I kick into its frictional heat, that divine
surface tension. Longing moves

like the water, and past the tour boat's
helm, I see it — a dolphin, face

under algae's skin, intimacy before
the ocean takes it back. I search

the eyes like jags of magma until
we become mirrors: the muscular

torso swiveling before torquing
into a sun-blessed dark. When

my mother was dying, I prayed
for a child to blossom in my body

where cancer had come, her womb
tumor-ravaged, cut out by

a surgeon. I longed to exchange
her pain for one I could

believe in — a child cresting
in me, love's sleek animal,

and she would live in the torrent
my body made for her. That year,

no child took root in me
like some creature of the deep.

No child surged from my grief-
lush body like love seized open.

But the dolphin? I watch it
bury itself in the spume.

Elegy for the Color Pink

I

I never imagined rock beneath the Sahara could be so cloying—
the color of bubble gum lush with spit, that first urgency of sugar—
but for millions of years, cyanobacteria fossils hushed up their beauty
in layers of dark earth. Before algae or the destiny of our ecosystem,
pink ruled the ocean. Pink ruled the earth. The oldest color shades
my cat's paws like pale adzuki beans. The oldest color, mauve
lipstick varnishing the butt of my mother's Benson & Hedges
menthol. Even now, when African dust blows through my city,
the color rushes my lungs.

II

Four, and I tore my Minnie Mouse bathing suit while climbing
the hood of my mother's car. Tired of my wading pool, dried dog shit,
and dandelions, that paint-baked four-door was a metal mountain
yearning to be touched. I climbed and slid, burning my thighs until
my suit caught on the windshield wiper, and my mother yelled for me
to *get the fuck down*. Years later, all I see is that wisp of nylon
martyring the rusted blade.

III

I'm still searching for it, a name for the young field mouse I rescued
from our backyard ant mound before I knew I couldn't save anyone.
Thin as a skinned persimmon, the translucent veins in her eyelids
pulsed. I thought of how her mother, still soft from birthing, must
have awakened to a rush of antennae, an army of insurgents taking
her. She refused the eyedropper full of milk I pushed at her mouth.

She twisted on my mother's hot water bottle, shit frothing from her
tail. Scared she would die in pain, I threw her out of the shotgun
window on the way to school. Sometimes, when I close my eyes,
I still see her body, the wind's rush and grip. Blood flecking
the asphalt with momentary heat, that pink.

IV

Once, I heard color referred to as *a loss of innocence,* as if color
could awaken us. For Homer, even the sea was *wine dark,*
the darkest pulse of pink possible. I'm trying to say something about
my mother's face when bilirubin thickened her blood, her liver
duct stent collapsed by tumors. Homer must have settled on *wine
dark* to describe the sea because no reference to blue existed in
the *Odyssey,* and his whole system of color was a kaleidoscope of errors:
violet sheep in the fields. Green honey. If my mother were a color,
I'd call her *winter-killed lemon on the verge of sunset.* It is true—
there was no record of blue until the ancient Egyptian texts,
but pink has always existed in the pulse of the brine.

V

When I think of color, I think of the linguist who never pointed
at the sky, the word *blue* an incantation lifting from his lips.
The famous experiment—to study how naming a color conjures
it to sight. When he asked his daughter Alma on a perfect day
in March—*What color is the sky?*—it took months for her to answer.
Blue, as in *the primary color between green and violet in the visible
spectrum,* as in *a wavelength between 450 and 500 nanometers.*
The world suddenly conspiring into order. One word enables
the blueness of blue, just as one word enables the pinkness of pink,
or my mother—whose skin still blazes in my dreams like flecks of light
off a wine-dark sea—enables the intimacy of that holy water.

Once, I Prayed in the Water

Lake Hanson, South Dakota

Blessed be the good-time girl   thigh-deep   in a striped inner tube
cattail fronds & cigarette butts   rough against her toes   blessed be
the empress of chic I was   sixteen   shellacked in Coppertone
tangled in a pick-up game   of football   my hands   muscular birds
gripping deep   through blitz   & tackle   all the jacked-up Fords
like drunk cicadas   pulsing hymns   through rolled-down windows
Stevie Ray & the Boss   shredding through steam   as I spread
my hips   my legs   & lunged   I was the girl kissing boys   in sit-on-top
kayaks   another flea-chawed dog   sun-blissed & brined   as if
someone told her   *Hey* pretty baby   *it's time to blow*
this mortal coil   every minute of her life   so I rode the twist & flush
of summer   until even the stars   couldn't look at me   before I
was a woman   *sand-hardened*   *late thirties*   I slid like a fish
into spume   I quaked all night   in the weeds   I fed on every shine
that would touch me   so *Lord*, will you make a temple   of the water
will you   brandish your body   in lake skin for me   I've had
enough of this   lemon-swoon sfumato   this musk-blaze of summer
genuflecting   like a fool   I've already buried   the shameless
pretty young thing   I was   I smoked that queen   when I kissed my mother
ravished by cancer   watched strange men   hoist her body
into an oven   set to the temperature   all things beautiful   begin to burn

Woman in Flames

Your body
Hurts me as the world hurts God. I am a lantern—

— Sylvia Plath

Call me lantern, not woman.
Heat beats my skin. It's almost pretty—
the ridges of my body sprung and stretched, as a star
inside me explodes, or is it a world?

Heat beats my skin. It's almost pretty,
my breath's trigger of ether
(exploding, or is it a world?).
The flicker of my little pain flower

(*my breath's trigger of ether*),
how it shoots, unroots through my legs
(the flicker of my little pain flower).
The fire swaggering its anger

through me shoots, unroots—
like a goddess, I'm turned out.
The fire swaggers its anger.
I'm flint, hot spit. Acetylene queen,

I'm a goddess turned out.
The ridges of my body, sprung and stretched.
I'm flint, hot spit. Acetylene queen,
Call me lantern, not woman.

The Boy

Heroin hushed through my first love's blood like sweet
pools in the throat of ripe honeysuckle. Seventeen, his heart
    unribboned
in the dark. Overdosed, you could almost hear it—*God*
calling the body back. His lips were petals bruising the dark.
I touched his skin until cool slicked
away every heat: *my first loss.* Years later, I'm lost

like someone still reentering the world. Loss,
I hold it like a lover. At my husband's school, the air is sweet
with threats: *I'll shoot up the school,* ink slicks,
sinister words ribboned
on the bathroom urinal. What makes a child go dark?
When a boy shot up a school three hours from us, they said God

unleashed his animal heart. They said, *God,*
deliver us from ourselves. A boy, lost,
after all, is not a killer unfurling in the dark.
Something lingers beneath him, some sweet,
brash hunger, some ribbon-
smooth call for help. When a girl forsakes him, must he slick

his anger into her? I want to hold the last slick
of shame his body can muster: Santa Fe ISD. Bullets studding
    Shana Fisher as God
calls her home. What is love when a bullet unribbons
a body? Parkland, Florida: a valentine lost
on the dash of a teacher's Honda Civic—pink sweetening
the interior, hearts. X's. O's. Darkness

is his body gunned down in front of a classroom. Darkness
like slicks
of gasoline surging through him, that sweet
diesel aura reaching down. I don't want to say *God*
every time a child kills. I don't want to lose
myself all night or ribbon

every victim together. I can't unribbon
the fear that lashes around me. When the dark
velvets us, I can barely touch my husband. My lost
sleep tilting into visions—*a child aiming his piece at him, gun
        metal slick
against smoke.* God,
let me unsee it—*his body falling forward, his rust-sweet*

blood misting the walls. The shooter, ribboned
by adrenaline, his jeans dark as bruised sugar. Once, I loved a boy
I couldn't save. I called out for God when he touched me.

God, You Are a Muscadine

Lord   your sweet is sharp-husked   a hymn slipped   over
    a battery
of seeds   to sow   I can see them   untrussed
    beneath
your rupture of sugar   *Lord*   you've tethered me   to that
    heaven of soothing
I've bitten through every mercy   to get to it   but you are
    the stone *(which stone?)*
in the dark   *Lord*   the pit   in my husband's kidney
    its whorl on the MRI
fixed into crystal   and I'm thinking   how in the bathroom
    Lord
he was like a boy   my husband   arched around the toilet   when
    I snatched him up
all bear hug and fisted collar   wrestled him   puking   into
    my car
ER nurses   threaded his veins with needles   anointed his chest
    with monitors
unleashed an IV drip   of morphine   into his blood   it was hours
    until
the three-millimeter mine   at the center of his kidney
    was snitched out   little coup
of calcium   set to bivouac his urethra   its plan to rage   through
    his sweet shaft
until the stone crested loose   yes   to translate the stone
    in my husband's kidney
is to translate a world   unknown to me   I think of the cells
    in my mother's body
how cancer slunk   between lymph   and vessel   like
    a thief

cancer drifting fugitively   through the skein of capillary   after
   capillary
my mother   made a force by   her father's   my
   father's hands
so skilled was she   at sassing disaster   when I said   *Some-*
   thing's wrong
when I said the word *doctor*   she came at me   what I mean
   is   she was not   my mother
but an animal   slashing   delirious until I shut my mouth
   but my husband
Oh Lord   I shunted his body   into my car   no alibi   could
   blunt that pain
radiating out of him   because my love   is sharp-husked
   as yours, *Lord*
another hymn of hardness   that could   begin   or end a world
   like you   *like you*
Lord, if you're thinking   of taking him   if you're
   dead set
on carrying him   into an air   other than mine   you'll
   have to drown me
in a sea of locusts   you'll have to *batter my heart*   *Lord*   you'll
   have
to kill me   if you want   to carry him home

Still Life with Smoke

Everywhere I go, my heart is hijacked
by menthol, my mother's hoodoo

a satin siren, an effigy stretching
its lost body sheer through my lungs.

Calla-shaped, her petals pilfer
a dusky exodus so hard and fast

I believe a tumor in my brain is the root
of this olfactory seizure of the soul,

some cellular malware eliciting
her lapsed kingdom come.

It started with dreams. Weeks after
she died, a field of petals, flies

clung as if to the skin of a plum.
In another, liver necrosis

tarnishing her face to nude ochre,
as if cancer were a girl smitten

with a spray can's reckless bliss,
a train depot, this child offering up

her namesake in strokes of graffiti.
Now, smoke like a fox's tail lacing

through grass. Smoke like a pleasure
instead of mercy. Always some

rupture of body and air. The last
time I saw her alive, I could smell

her tumors ulcerating, that honey-
crust stink of a wound already

damned. But now? She's minx-heady,
a flux in the heat. She's silt.

What's left of her body—I'm taken.
I'm steeped.

Elegy with Blueberries

After Seamus Heaney

Afterward, everything
felt June-braised, root-fed,

heat under the skin
like some dark sugar

thrashed and curled.
It felt absurd, the world

ripening so shamelessly—
black-eyed Susans sleek

in the ditches, sawflies
devouring the plush

velvety heads. They remind
me of blueberries,

heat ripping through
the sun-bleached pulp.

As a child, I flung
the unripe—still like

rabbit eyes—onto
the ground. Now, I savor

the turgor in each snap,
too sharp and brief

to be called agonal.
Little deaths, want

eulogizing want until
tart lightning burns me.

When she died,
her blood clotted dark

with bilirubin. The coma
turned her to berry,

sun flickering through
her. When I was small,

I took for granted
the inky knots still vine-

smitten at season's
end. Now, I slip

their heat-slick wounds
into my mouth, as if

any blue could sing
right through me.

Death Buried the Daughter I Was

I talk to the ghosts holding vigil in my house,
because I am a child still burying my dead.

> Death buried the daughter I was.
> *Daughter*, a gardenia milking the sun-sick earth.

My mother swore the season's first gardenia
was proof she'd live, though cancer bloomed

> through her skin. Proof, when nothing
> came to her garden. I knew it was the end

when she let her garden go. Chicken hawks dragging bones
in a lapsed orchard—that was the smell of cancer eating her.

> That smell—chicken trucks blazing the road.
> Shit lacing the feathers of the damned.
> ～

In the hospital, my husband talks to God
all night. He wakes with fear on his breath.

> He wakes with fear on his breath, acid
> spiking his blood. Doctors call it *ketoacidosis*.

His blood, death-spiked. Doctors threaten ICU.
I ask my husband not to die tonight.

> We all die a little bit every night.
> I heard my mother's last breath swell

above her oxygen tank—my mother's last breath.
Her body sang its eulogy as her soul let go.

    I sang her eulogy as I let her soul go.
    At the funeral home, I kissed her.

Grief on my breath,
       I'm still kissing her.
     ~

The first time we shot up my husband
at home, I triggered the needle.

    I triggered the needle, injecting
    his bicep with insulin. Once, a bee stung

my bicep at the end of our cul-de-sac.
A honeybee shot her stinger into my skin.

    Stinger in my skin, she entered me.
    Afraid of my pain, I beat her out of the sky.

Fear made me beat her. I didn't know bees, born
mouthless, live in endless hunger.

    Imagine it—hunger, then your belly
    ripped from its stinger. And I killed her.

I'm ripped from my trigger.
I talk to the ghosts holding vigil in my house.

What the Time-Share Man at the Westgate Hotel Tried to Sell Me

Las Vegas, Nevada

A flash, then metal hurling
into him. He woke bleeding out
in the sun-slapped ditch.

*How many vacations do you
think you have left?* he asks.
He wants to sell me weeks

leased in a shared villa
in Branson or Orlando.
He says it was a hit-and-run.

Once, I rode a bus
with my husband to visit
the Grand Canyon, to watch

ice choke the gorge's rim.
Juniper jutted from river-cut plateaus
that could pierce the sky

or shunt their weight
to the thrusting Colorado.
I hung my legs over

the edge, ice melting
through my jeans, my thighs
gripping at the chill.

Once, my mother cut
herself washing dishes, watched
blood ribbon into water

like something gracious
and good. It curled into itself,
as if to float for a moment,

then disappeared into its own
shame of being, like she wished
to curl—her naked palm

rising against the water's
steam. The lie she hadn't meant
to do it. Even water forced

its mercy into her—
the way a river will hurry
into shifting rock,

will smooth any jagged
space that will have it. The way
that my husband, eager

for lodge fire and spice-
flushed cider, lifts me,
laughing, into his arms.

III

Terra Nova

Parting is all we know of heaven,
And all we need of hell.

—Emily Dickinson

God owns heaven
but He craves the earth.

—Anne Sexton

Terra Nova

I

What one calls hijinks, another calls gospel,
    like Hemingway jotting six words on a napkin—
        For sale: baby shoes. Never worn. This is how novels

        are born. Six-word stories. I believe in whimsy,
    the uncanny cells that bind us. Blood jets rendering
a story smooth. *Mother died too young. Miss her.*

Still missing her. No more words.
    Imagine this heroine, black down to her underwear.
    She's Mothra incognito, winged girl

        cresting through calamity like another
    stage of grief. Tell me you'd watch her dark night
of the soul, breathless as she splits her cocoon.

        Hard as jade, tell me you could love her. You could
pity her story until another genre explodes.

II

Pity her story, its genre exploding. When my mother said,
    Love is how you suffer together, I heard *Marry the nice boy,*
        not the boy you'd rather fuck. I heard *Love is the welt*

        a boy always leaves, thumbprints like ghosts of blackberries.
    I didn't marry the nice boy, Mother. I'm still breathing
in the love you always feared, how sudden it is,

how ugly it can be when it unsutures its hold—
    yellow-green love like the moon in heat. Crescent, waxing,
        half-illumined gibbous love, or the moon-is-always-
            turning-vascular

    kind of love. In other words, love undoing itself,
    seeking a center. Forgive me, Mother, when I mean to say—
Love forms my body's reckless galaxy. Make of me

    love's natural order, when I mean to say,
when I mean to say—*My body: where do I end?*

III

My body: where do I end? I'm five. She's cutting sharp
    into a Winn-Dixie parking lot, our car sideswiped by a sedan.
        Her torso struck with the airbag's punch.

    Glass in my face. A whole history fractured in that moment
    hanging, limboed by heat, another spring glitzing
through fissure, the lilt of car exhaust—I said—*My body:*

where do I end? How long until her voice
    is a hush I can't recall? I used to map the scars
        on her hands, the windshield's fractal tattooing

    her palms. Hot oil feathering.
    She called it a luna moth, the scar eclipsing
her thumb and index finger, the pulsing spot.

    Evidence we can be erased. As if to say,
In her end is my beginning.

IV

Begin me, IV drip of morphine,
    Stanley Cup playoffs on the TV
        Nurse Linda rigs toward her hospice bed.

    Begin me, Penguins winning the series 4–2.
    Begin me, liver necrosis dropping its gloves,
hoisting her past the final scrimmage. My mother, the trophy

refracting. Begin me, circle that will not end.
    Begin me, wound never closing. If love
        shifts within us, begin here, as if

    longing is a verb. Her oxygen tank
on the La-Z-Boy, her breath's rasping engine.
I want love as strong as this cellular chain.

    If love must break us, begin here, Mother —
is it the world or your blood still clenching me?

        V

Is it the world or your blood still clenching? When you died,
    Mother, I stopped eating. Nothing could force
        its way inside me. On bad days, I dream

    I'm the darkest hole your body left.
    On better ones, I'm tearing Sunbeam bread
for gulls in my dreams. I'm breathing in salt, cracked shell.

Those years, I watched you in your strapless one-piece
    turn golden under a hymn of oil. You'd rub
        aloe where the skin peeled, a blister's

glitz-born violence in your skin. Planets,
not freckles, unhusking your epithelial heat.
How can all of this exist in a cloisonné urn?

I envy the ghost-gulls, their bodies lunging
toward every sliver. Pilgrims, they feast on ether.

VI

She came, my mother, like a pilgrim of ether.
A portent, awoken, in a glitter of yellow.
Yellow rendezvous as I spoke my vows.

Yellow, slinking like a clade of wasps.
You could hear her blatant murmur against my throat,
her risk getting handsy with the small of my back. Every fleur-de-lis

within reach, graffitied by our lady of the torrent: Yellow,
yellow everywhere. A piss-bright heat.
My husband whispered: *Your mother's with us,*

and her ghost is raising hell. Pity my rhinestone tiara,
my glass of prosecco. Even the cake was spiked —
nothing survived her blaze. For an RSVP,

my mother preached her gripes. In every picture,
I'm a flash of torched vanilla. I radiate.

VII

If I could hawk you six words smooth as snake oil,
I'd quote the Gospel of Grief. I'd deliver a sermon:
Six words can preach, bear witness. Their spirit can testify!

I'd doctor you sequels with names like *A Story After the World Ended*
or *Lovely Apocalypse: A Whole New Normal,* until their Hail
Marys vibrate your blood: *Things are okay.*

Every lost daughter would abandon her loop of shame—
     Mother, forgive me—and save herself. This is my story.
          An eight-pound tumor raged through my mother's colon,

          zigzagged through her uterine walls.
     Her ovaries, synchronous metastases.
Emergency surgery. Doctors cut it

          out of her, that little death baby.
When she died on the table, they shocked her back to life.

                    VIII
Oh mother who died on the table, oh mother of the failed liver,
     oh mother of the tumors fruiting in the dark.
          Begin again. *Oh mother of wild persimmons*

          in her liver ducts, oh mother of harvest starring her lungs.
     Again. *Oh mother of the last bowel movement*
less shit than blood, oh mother of the BiPAP mask,

oh mother of the living room hospital bed,
     oh mother of the coma. As if to say—*oh mother*
          of the last meal, oh mother who no longer

          drinks water, she's too busy drinking the last of God
     from the air. It happens this way, the body a color
radiating blatantly: *love tongue, mother tongue,*

as if to say—*I'm a puddle of light.*
Or, between tongue and glottal stop—*holy.*

IX
Dear Mother, I'm ashamed. I've forgotten what's holy.
        The past is hijinks, not blood jets. Death wore me smooth.
        People say we look alike when a picture snaps me

                with my head thrown back, my laugh all horse teeth and sass.
        And sometimes, a pull off of an unfiltered cigarette
and you're here like hard jade, another dark night of the soul.

Sometimes, I dream of your steel-blue eyes, wake up
        with them instead of my own. Which is to say, *God*
                is the geometry guiding our mercy. I want to say *love*

                is the cigarette smoke haunting a heaven without you
        in six words. To win a bet like Hemingway.
To master what's never been mine. So I say—*The dusky*

        half-life is most familiar. Mother. *Mother.*
Even the name obliterates me.

IV

Terra Firma

But there are moments, walking, when I catch a glimpse of myself in the
*   window glass,*
say, the window of the corner video store, and I'm gripped by a cherishing
*   so deep*

for my own blowing hair, chapped face, and unbuttoned coat that I'm
*   speechless:*
I am living, I remember you.

—Marie Howe

Terra Firma

I sink my heels into darkness, that silky tether.
Grief is an island of mercy touching my skin.
It hurts like hell to bury your mother.

Longing is my other story—not cancer,
not coma hushing her into its dirty hymn.
I sink my heels into darkness, that silky tether.

Too wicked to die, I thought she'd live forever.
She seethed all night on cigarettes and gin.
It hurts like hell to bury your mother.

I swallowed her storm, as if love was duty, not weather.
Surges, riptides braising my heart with her din.
I sink my heels into darkness, that silky tether.

I hated the menthol scenting her black leather
jacket. I still tangle my body up in its sensuous sin.
It hurts like hell to bury your mother.

What is pain but a story of mercy? It lingers
in my blood. All things end to end again.
I sink my heels into darkness, that silky tether.
It hurts like hell to bury your mother.

Last Stash

When I say I busted
    my mother's stash in the Deep
                -freeze meant for flash sales,
                    I mean I snuffed out their cool
hushed up against Styrofoam
    flats of cube steak, I mean
                I snitched on their glitzy foil.
                  For years, I watched my mother
grip them between her
    lips. I watched her throat
                their mirth like an indulgence
                  too holy to blame. When I say
she'd smoke until the moon
    glistened raw as her lungs,
                I mean she'd smoke until her
                  body became a savior lost.
After her stroke, she quit—
    but the stash nestled
                behind the Girl Scout
                  Thin Mints for the moment
all hope was lost?
    Imagine her heaven
                paved with cartons,
                  the pearly gates roached out
with haze. *Terminal* meant
    a litter of filters
                christened with lipstick
                and ashed.
When she died, this sorry
    klatch hustled itself deep,

a lone coterie of stale
bones. When I say, *There but for*
the grace of God go I, I mean
I'm grappling the last pack
like a bastard angel
of mercy. I mean I'm pitching
its low-down sack
of a soul into the trash.

Traitor Angels

Two days, two nights we pearl
together, thrash, our bodies twin engines

rash and seething. If God is here,
sleeping in the thrall, let Him shimmer

through the walls. Let Him come
to us, raging. I'm too radiant for paradise.

Angels are unthinkable in hot weather,
unless they are hell-bent raiders

hard-flung and bestial. When our AC
seized in the August roil, the run

capacitor a failed tsunami of jolts,
compressor blades churning, it must

have been angels, their ash-glitzed
fury moving them. When the technician

comes, restores the dead capacitor,
the compressor hums as if reborn.

I imagine them, the traitor angels,
leaping from my windows,

burrowing back through layers
of dirt, as if luscious and spent,

they were only boys, and it was
their mother, not the devil,

calling and calling them home.

Mercy Villanelle

Rusk, Texas

Pine roots flare in the ditch and I see a heart—
whorls of vena cava lush with rain.
To heal the soul is a scientific art.

Rain rushes in like a fool, a jagged arc.
Needles purl in the ditch. The stars are spume.
Pine roots flare in the ditch and I see a heart.

We shoot through lanes in the pitch-black dark.
A woman grows bored with the man in the moon.
To heal the soul is a scientific art.

I'm a moth curled in a French drain, awakened.
I'll savor you, husband, like lemon crushed into gin.
Pine roots flare in the ditch and I see a heart.

A barn owl shrieks like a man crying out.
Even the wind is jilted. It whips and blooms.
To heal the soul is a scientific art.

Take me until the moon, that fool, burns out.
Take me like the dead-dog storm unhinges.
Pine roots flare in the ditch and I see a heart.
To heal the soul is a scientific art.

Elegy in the Shape of a River

Livingston, Texas

If faith is a river, I am the red-eared slider turtle,
algae-smudged, ducks feasting from my shell.

I am the flame-throated jill, little boat of feathers,
gnawing at spores with my bill. Years ago,

I gnawed at hope like dusk giving up
its clutch, peach slit, indigo hardening the sky.

Now, stars slit the sky hard.
Now, I watch stones thrown from the pipe dock.

I watch the river, rock-stunned, the child, now
running toward his mother's voice, the way animals

panic in the wake of any small violence. When I lost
the baby, I watched love like violence shimmer,

linger a moment, then let go. Yes, shimmer—
as if faith is a river. As if faith is a river.

Weather Haibun

The storm was demoted to a winter advisory, but your father still
urged us to hang back until noon. At the Iowa border, hail like BB
pellets, sleet clinging to the windshield in gasps. Then snow fuming
over soybean fields, grain elevators, pelts of cattle and horses. By
Omaha, snow obscured the edges of things, softened them as dusk
came on. Our tires skidded over brine-treated roads. Wind thrashed
your face when we stopped to pump gas. We locked eyes through
the window, snow clotting into your beard like a hardened kiss. Ice
spread until cold was an imagined place we settled down into, no
choice but to accept the fact of it surging into us.

~

I'm thinking of your father, his warning tone born from years
hauling load. The storm had socked in his mobile home within
an hour. Because we called the city office between dead spots,
complaining he was divorced, elderly, couldn't get his truck out of
the garage, the Parks Department sent a worker on a four-wheeler
hitched up with a snowplow, drifts from the curb flash frozen into a
wall of ice. *No luck trying to lift it,* he said. *Hard as granite, the son
of a bitch will stay that way to first thaw.*

~

Winter is not something to fear—your words, husband, not mine.
You'll wreck on the road. You'll never leave home. Respect winter,
you always said: glide into turns, let the cut made by others' tires
lift you to traction. If you respect your enemy, your enemy will
have no choice but to respect you. I've driven through my share of
whiteouts, subzero swaths of midwestern freeze. Flurries where the
moon illuminates ice, a milky sheen feathering the darkness. I've
seen ethanol plants unleash their steam like breath, followed it like

a compass of smoke. But I grew up in heat, thunder lilting through the air. I grew up with rain lifting me onto the skin of water, my foot triggering the break. I grew up speaking the language of hydroplane, learning to drive into slurries of water, to lean into beauty that could kill me. I learned to trust the slippery collusion and cohesion, boundaries shifting as I fought the sleek path to higher ground.

～

When a cloud-lashed sky unshelters its anger—then rain, manic, squalls its raw love down. Tires deep, flood-martyred, I pulse my breaks and glide. Everything wet-spun, metal throating diesel. Dusk coming with its little wolf mouth. Stars flashing. Two Julys ago, I rode the highway's shoulder, I-40, grafted between semis. We could have slow-danced all night like this, bumper to bumper, our heat entangled until the next hard stop. *Don't stop.* I'll never give myself to some glazed-up convoy, windshield kissing me open, glass in my mouth. I won't hold the airbag like a lover, give my body to its nylon surge. To outrun the storm, I'll drive straight into darkness. Think of it—the other car cutting lanes, how it hydroplaned, fishtailed. The driver jagging the wheel, spinning out. His eyes flashing, fear live-wiring out of him. We almost crash before he trips the ditch, flips. Like a cat sunning, belly stretched toward the air. His roof caves. His rust-mangled engine seethes. A man is his story of darkness. My story? *I lived.*

～

During every tornado, I'm thinking of stars. Pilger, Nebraska, 2014. The meteorologist called them sisters, funnels grafted to the same spine of rotating air, but I knew they were lovers by how my jet turned wet and reckless between squalls, by how the squalls seemed raptured from the same nexus of desire. But I was thinking of your hands on my body, not the storm. On our way to the airport, cottonwoods thronged across asphalt, their catkins clinging to each tire's underbelly, while power lines helixed, sinuous, in slicks of rain. Haven't we all known darkness like this? The kind requiring a wind-up radio, that ends with the only clear station reporting news of destroyed silos, missing children? The kind the plane taking me away from you tried to rise through but, overcome, turned instead to a gale's handfast ceremony—luggage breaching the cargo hold, a woman's head quick and loose against the plane's thermoplastic wall? As my plane, not felled but wounded, hunted for any runway that would have it, I thought of last summer's solstice, the man who coaxed us toward his telescope, promising Saturn's curves, rings enticing a sure liaison with Mars. As he thumbed the focusing knob, as I squinted into the eyepiece, Libra's quadrangle hid away. Saturn gave her body to the dark. As I feared the forces that begin and end our bond to everything, you only kissed me like a tempest plunges itself into the border of a larger vortex. We were not yet married, husband. You wouldn't stop kissing me.

~

New Year's Eve 2013, we left a party in the middle of a whiteout. Your two-wheel drive skidded at each farm-to-market intersection. Wasted on Tempranillo, I imagined the storm was a rollercoaster fishtailing us. *At least we'll die together,* I said. Laughed until you stopped shushing me, warning me fate would land us wheels-up in a ditch. Until you were laughing too, palm on my thigh, sliding into the crushed ice passing for your apartment's driveway. Until we kissed and kissed, finally killing the engine, our breath curlicuing like ghosts. It became a joke that stuck—*at least we'll die together.* You told me that any girl crazy enough to die in the snow with you would make one hell of a wife.

~

As we go east this time, the storm lashes, thermostat dropping from 71 degrees in Texas to 50 off the Oklahoma turnpike, urging us to *drive friendly* and not to *drive into the smoke.* Haven't we always driven into the smoke together—my mother's death, your brother's

multiple sclerosis, miscarriage, your mother vanishing after our
wedding, her silence the closest consolation to goodbye? Teach me
to savor the weather in your skin. I'll careen off the road of you, hit
hard into your chest like a drift. My engine will stall in your chill.
Shiver me into that final warmth.

∿

Surging past dead space,
careening without friction,
    we are weightlessness.

They Call Her Mi Corazon

Though her shelter name
is inked into manila, lapsed letters
on an intake form. Under
the rendezvous of newspaper strips,
she's Ouroboros, incessant goddess
of bleached steel. The women
who work here, you can tell
they picked through her coat
with their nails — her flea-sloughed
body coaxed to flax, cream-gray
whorls spinning in the room's
fluorescent light. Her eyes flare
with the ecstasy of the nearly
damned — ochre slits, dilated irises
flickering. They say the sheriff
found her slinking in a ditch,
held her against his body to warm her.
Never hungry, her bones jut dangerously
as I palm her haunches, lift until
my mother's death stops calling
to me. I sign papers, drive
the rain-striated streets to the rhythm
of her throat calls. Home, she angles
her body under the daybed, slashes
at tendrils of dust with her claws.
Vets call it *shelter shock*, the trauma
of moving between differing versions
of reality — harsh metal, the snarls
of ferals killed on arrival, then someone
not your mother calling your name.

We are the prodigal ones —
cat milking the blanket's effigy,
God taking another baby from my womb.
Sisters in sorrow, the kind that
reterritorializes destiny. What could
have been. What is no longer.
Mi Corazon — in the orchard of love,
she thickens, belly a curling
rind of cantaloupe. Now, she would
kill for the woman who feeds her.

My Mother Comes Back as a Dragonfly

I swear I saw   a cool moon heat   some angel reborn
in carnival glass   she was throwing shade from the junk store window
strung out on fishing twine   some kitsch bird-of-paradise
some tchotchke mama   flaunting a luminous   vintage thorax
I watched her   pivot   all done up with light   her compound eyes
twin disco balls   I still want the jewel tones   glinting from her spine
to blow the sky open   I want the blaze   that means the dead
no longer haunt   the coordinates of our world   and if we say
the dead are only intransitive   do they still seek a signifier?
My mother   died five Mays ago   and I'm locking eyes with glass
some dime-store effigy   hocked on clearance   I'm chump enough
to believe   still holds her   some hoodoo grace   you could call it
steeping every memory   I revise here as though   wanting a thing
could make the act   (of wanting it)   simpler   than touch   Once I
couldn't stop searching   for the sheer breach of it   on my grandmother's
persimmon tree   the naked devotion   of simply witnessing
(*does that make it simple?*)   a carapace slit open   a ghost-colored interloper
easing its wings   from the breathing sarcophagus   knitted to a branch
I watched the old eyes   go dead   but you could say   it was lovely
the belly downright swindled   from its old skin   the muscles in the thorax
all shiver   and blind urge   you could say   I was watching a spirit   jettison
from its last-known instar   gussy itself up   for flight   my mother
once said   dragonflies are the spirits   of our lost ones   returned to us
that when her grandfather died   they thronged in swarms   by the mailbox
the juniper garden just lit up   with them   *like stars*   she said
that would land in her braid   churn their wings   with such fury
she couldn't unhear   the rusted-bicycle-spoke sound of it   until she
was persuaded   that every iridescent body   is a soul come home
it is said   that the dragonfly nymph   is a predator underwater
and because science is shameful   its flight cycle lasts weeks

not years   but these facts   don't stop me from trusting
that the dead need stories   to keep them iridescent   *yes*   my mother
comes back to me   but not like eggs   on the sheen of water
a version of herself feeding in the dark   she does not perch
on persimmon trees   to sass the spirit   twisting out of her   last-known body
she does not shimmy her wings   just to show off   a reckoning
much stronger than silk   I'm trying to say   that glimmer haunting me
at the junk store window   is a fool's errand   some hoax omen   I can't
talk myself out of believing   I'm sorry   the dazzle of someone else's
lost splendor   brings me to my knees   when I say that angel
was the winged thing   slipped out of my mother   I'm only saying
my mother is dead

Cherishing

History has to live with what was here,
as if Here, a jilted lover, won't get gone.
Here, clutched up on me, lays its shattered spoon
of a body down. Why Here, not There?

There, like a safe word even God won't use.
There, it's never dark when destruction turns,
when the sky burns open, and, heron-slick,
the future waits. I'm so damn sick of Here,

its storm of jokes and nerves, its fatal hope.
My true north led me straight to Then's end,
strung-out effigy of the infinite.
How can I live like this and truly live?

The world is salt, then breath. Breath, then birth.
Here, get gone now. Give me back to the earth.

Winter Gazebo

Madison, South Dakota

The sky, it's full of ghosts.
When we married here, azaleas swung from
the ceiling joists. Our vows hung low,

my body singed by their earthy haunt.
Love, it beat itself into the shingles. We had not yet
made metaphors for what would

clench its story between us
in another season—icicle lights flashing such fire,
Christmas wreaths wretched

as iridescent fruit. If light enters ice,
ghostlike, it arrows back. Once, gussied up in lace,
I fell into us. Azalea crush.

Desire, I thought, was the end.
Now, wind-lashed, we lean on rails. We are past joy,
past that feral elegy calling to us.

Our shadows entangle,
make love in the snow, as if love could
bruise us beautiful.

Acknowledgments

I extend my gratitude to the following publications in which earlier versions of these poems first appeared: the *Account*, *Big Muddy*, *Concho River Review*, *Connotation Press*, *Crab Orchard Review*, *Minnesota Review*, *Oakwood*, *Paterson Literary Review*, Poetry Society of America Online, *Rappahannock Review*, *Roanoke Review*, *South Dakota in Poems* (South Dakota State Poetry Society), *Stirring*, *Superstition Review*, *Tahoma Literary Review*, *Tupelo Quarterly*, *Valparaiso Poetry Review*, the *West Review*, and *Wild Gods: The Ecstatic In Contemporary Poetry and Prose* (New Rivers Press).

I offer my gratitude to Khaled Mattawa for choosing "Terra Inferna," "My Mother Comes Back as a Dragonfly," "Once, I Prayed in the Water," and "Last Stash" as winners of the 2019 George Bogin Memorial Award from the Poetry Society of America.

I offer my gratitude to Maria Mazziotti Gillan for choosing "Weather Haibun" as first prize cowinner of the 2020 Allen Ginsberg Poetry Award, sponsored by the Poetry Center at Passaic County Community College.

This book would not exist without the support of Ohio University Press, the Sewanee Writers' Conference, Stephen F. Austin State University, the Poetry Society of America, and the Poetry Center at Passaic County Community College. I offer my gratitude to general editor Sarah Green, contest judge Rebecca Morgan Frank, and everyone at Ohio University Press for turning this dream of a book into reality. I offer profound gratitude to A. E. Stallings and to Mark Jarman for their transformative feedback on individual poems, as well as for offering pivotal advice for the manuscript's conceptual framework. Sewanee is a special place, and I will always hold my Sewanee family—Bob Hass, Pete Fairchild, Mary Jo Salter,

Marilyn Nelson, Chad Abushanab, Joe Capista, Armen Davoudian, Terry Blackhawk, Michael Mark, Natalie Staples, Conor Bracken, Jacklyn Dwyer, Mary Ann O'Gorman, A. R. Johnson, Bonnie Naradzay, Chelsea Whitton, Will Rankin, Alexis Sears, Eli Burrell, Alyse Bensel, Emily Koehn, Laura Murphy, Chelsea Rathburn, Edgar Kunz, and Jim May, among others—close to my heart. I offer my deepest gratitude to Maggie Smith and to Heather Dobbins, who offered powerful feedback on this manuscript. To Mark Sanders, Kimberly Verhines, and Sue Whatley—my SFA family—I offer heartfelt gratitude for being the family I can turn to in darkness and in light. Finally, I offer my loving gratitude to Matthew, sweet Matthew—our marriage is the earth I stand on.

Notes

"Terra Inferna" (3): The Latin title of this poem roughly means
"hell on earth." The poem refers to a true story concerning the
painter Joe Andoe. Decades after his high school girlfriend
died in a fire, he began to paint pastures filled with horses
and female nudes. The horses and nudes had one thing in
common: they were variations of the same horse and the same
woman. He came to understand that the obsessive images were
related to what he called "post-traumatic pleasure disorder,"
specifically concerning an image of beauty he often returned to
from his high school days: Playing hooky from school, he and
the girlfriend parked in a local field to have sex. Then, a wild
mare pushed her face into the car's window. He said that the
paintings must have been a reaction to losing the girlfriend and
the innocence crystallized in that moment, as the horse in the
paintings was the mare and the nudes all had the girlfriend's
face. The lines "a girl so lovely / it hurts to look at her" are
inspired by an exchange between Rickie, Rayanne, and Angela
from the pilot episode of the 1990s teen drama *My So-Called
Life*.

"Queening" (6): The details of the scientific mechanisms behind
microchimerism were collected from Vanessa Hua's article
"Your Baby's Leftover DNA Is Making You Stronger" (*Atlantic*,
October 20, 2014). The poem's title follows Jane Hirshfield's
poem "For What Binds Us," as well as Sandra Meek's poem
"The Ties That Bind Us."

"Elegy Beginning with the Birth of a Mountain" (10): Information
about the isoprene haze around the Blue Ridge Mountains
was taken directly from the article "What Makes the Smoky
Mountains Smoky?" (*Smoky Mountain News* [blog], Visit My

Smokies, April 26, 2016, https://www.visitmysmokies.com/blog/
smoky-mountains/what-makes-the-smoky-mountains-smoky/).
The image of the cow elk in the road first appears in Mark
Spragg's essay "My Sister's Boots" (in *Where Rivers Change
Direction* [New York: Riverhead Books, 1999]).

"Cancer" (15): Dilaudid (hydromorphone hydrochloride) is
an opioid analgesic used to control severe pain. One of its
potential serious side effects is hallucinations. The phrase "To
die, to sleep" comes from *Hamlet*.

"Here Be Dragons" (17): Abraham Ortelius's *Theatrum Orbis
Terrarum* (1570), the first modern atlas, often integrated
drawings of mythical creatures into its maps. The phrase "Here
be dragons" imitates such a practice and was used to designate
possibly dangerous uncharted territories. This poem references
Frank O'Hara's poem "In Memory of My Feelings," specifically
the lines: "When you turn your head / can you feel your heels,
undulating?" and "I haven't told you of the most beautiful
things / in my lives, and watching the ripple of their loss
disappear / along the shore, underneath ferns" (from section
5). The phrase "blazed up" comes from James Wright's poem
"Lying in a Hammock at William Duffy's Farm in Pine Island,
Minnesota."

"Terra Incognita" (21): *Terra incognita,* Latin for "unknown land," is
a term used by cartographers to describe terrains that have been
unmapped or otherwise undocumented. Though the term was
first witnessed in Ptolemy's *Geography*, a work repopularized
during the Age of Discovery (which began in the fifteenth
century), it lost its geographical mystique during the nineteenth
century, when all coastlines and continents had been charted.
This poem alludes to Matt Rasmussen's poem "A Horse Grazes
in My Shadow," particularly the lines "I wish the god of this
place / would put me in its mouth / until I dissolve, until / the
field doesn't end." The lines "Grief doesn't have a face like /

the living do" reference Marie Howe's poem (and eponymous collection) "What the Living Do."

"Elegy for the Color Pink" (23): The anecdote about linguist Guy Deutscher and his daughter Alma, the discussion of blue's absence in Homer's work, and the direct quotation regarding blueness take inspiration from a podcast episode titled "Colors" (*Radiolab*, May 21, 2012, produced by Tim Howard and Pat Walters). The following description refers to the scientific definition of blue: *the primary color between green and violet in the visible spectrum, as in a wavelength between 450 and 500 nanometers.*

"Once, I Prayed in the Water" (25): Several lines refer to Chris Abani's poem "God's Country": "All cremation ovens are set to / the temperature it takes to burn a heart. / It just won't die." Several lines also reference Flannery O'Connor's story "A Good Man Is Hard to Find," particularly the line "'She would've been a good woman,' The Misfit said, 'if it had been somebody there to shoot her every minute of her life.'"

"Woman in Flames" (26): This pantoum is an answer of sorts to Sylvia Plath's poem "Fever 103°." Plath's poem, written in the midst of illness, rages at the betrayal of her husband, Ted Hughes, who wronged her by leaving her for another woman. In my poem, the speaker sees herself mirrored in her mother's cremated body, raging, burning, and coming undone.

"The Boy" (27): On May 18, 2018, a school shooting occurred at Santa Fe High School in Santa Fe, Texas. Ten people were fatally shot and thirteen others were wounded. The gunman, seventeen-year-old Dimitrios Pagourtzis, was said to have made repeated advances on Shana Fisher, a classmate. Fisher's mother speculated that her daughter's rejection of Pagourtzis was one of the main catalysts for the school shooting. The mother claimed that her daughter was also the first shooting victim. On February 13, 2018, Gwen Gossler left a Valentine's Day card in her fiancée's car while he showered. The next day, her fiancée—high school geography teacher and cross-country coach Scott Beigel—was shot by an ex-student, nineteen-year-old Nikolas Cruz, in front of the door to his classroom while trying to save students. Beigel's death was part of the school shooting at Marjory Stoneman Douglas High School in Parkland, Florida, in which fourteen students and three staff members were fatally shot. Seventeen others were wounded, making the shooting one of the deadliest school massacres in American history. The poem owes much to Marie Howe's "The Gate," specifically the lines "I had no idea that the gate I would step through / to finally enter this world / would be the space my brother's body made."

"God, You Are a Muscadine" (29): The phrase "you'll have to *batter my heart*" references John Donne's "Holy Sonnets."

"Elegy with Blueberries" (33): This poem takes its inspiration from Seamus Heaney's poem "Blackberry-Picking."

"Terra Nova" (41): *Terra nova* is Latin for "new land." While Hemingway's six-word story is largely the stuff of urban legend, sources indicate that the origin of the six-word story could date back to as early as 1906. The following lines were taken from a conversation I had with Aldina Vazao Kennedy regarding my mother's first death anniversary: "*Mother died too young. Miss her. / Still missing her. No more words. /* Imagine this heroine, black down to her underwear." The references to blood jets summon Sylvia Plath's poem "Kindness," particularly the line "The blood jet is poetry." The line "*In her end is my beginning*" is indebted to T. S. Eliot's poem "East Coker," specifically the line "In my beginning is my end."

"Terra Firma" (49): *Terra firma* is Latin for "the earth under one's boots," or "the ground as distinct from the sea or air."

"Traitor Angels" (52): The line "Angels are unthinkable in hot weather" originates directly from Monica Youn's poem "A Parking Lot in West Houston."

"Mercy Villanelle" (54): The line "To heal the soul is a scientific art" comes from advice given to me by friend and fellow writer Sue Whatley.

"Elegy in the Shape of a River" (55): This poem's title is a loose adaptation of Jon Pineda's poem "Memory in the Shape of a Swimming Lesson."

"Cherishing" (64): This poem is a sonnenizio, Kim Addonizio's spin on the sonnet. As per the formal requirements, this poem begins with a line from Robert Lowell's sonnet "History."

"Winter Gazebo" (65): The opening line of the poem, "The sky, it's full of ghosts," was written in tribute to the following sentence from Jo Ann Beard's essay "The Fourth State of Matter": "The sky is full of dead men, drifting in the blackness like helium balloons."